The Anglican Family Prayer Book

The Anglican Family Prayer Book

ANNE E. KITCH

MP | Morehouse Publishing
NEW YORK · HARRISBURG · DENVER

Unless otherwise noted, the Scripture quotations contained herein are from the New Revised Standard Version Bible, copyright © 1989 by the Division of Christian Education of the National Council of Churches of Christ in the U.S.A. Used by permission. All rights reserved.

The psalms contained herein are from the Psalter in The Book of Common Prayer, copyright © 1979 by The Church Hymnal Corporation, New York

Excerpt from the Doxology by Michael Allen Burke. Reprinted by permission of the author.

Excerpts from The Book of Alternative Services of the Anglican Church of Canada.
Copyright © 1985 by the General Synod of the Anglican Church of Canada. Reprinted by permission of the Anglican Church of Canada.

The five blessings from "Blessing Over Food at Easter" are from The Book of Occasional Services 1994, pages 97-98, copyright © 1995 Church Pension Fund. Used by permission of Church Publishing.

Art by C.E. Visminis Co., Ltd.

Morehouse Publishing, 4775 Linglestown Road, Harrisburg, PA 17112

Morehouse Publishing, 445 Fifth Avenue, New York, NY 10016

Morehouse Publishing is an imprint of Church Publishing Incorporated.
www.churchpublishing.org

Library of Congress Cataloging-in-Publication Data

The Anglican family prayer book / [edited by] Anne E. Kitch.
p.cm.
Includes bibliographical references and index.
ISBN 978-0-8192-1940-4

1. Family—Prayer-books and devotions—English. 2. Anglican
Communion—Prayer-books and devotions—English. I. Kitch, Anne E.
BX5147.F35A54 2004
242'.803—dc21

2003005086

Printed in the United States of America

For Jack and Betsy Kitch

Acknowledgments

I am ever grateful to Debra Farrington at Morehouse for her support and our shared enthusiasm for nurturing faith that brought about this book. Thanks to Suzanne Guthrie for reading the manuscript and offering wise and gracious insights. And a special thanks to my husband, James Peck, with whom it is a joy to celebrate faith in our home.

Contents

ॐ Praying Through the Day

ॐ Prayers for People and Occasions

☿ Prayers for the Eucharist

ᵴ Prayers for the Church Year

Introduction

When I was a young child, we lived across the street from the church we attended, St. Michael and All Angels, in Colorado Springs. As a child, I found myself drawn to the empty church during the week. I would walk cautiously into the half-darkened space, enraptured by the silence and sense of mystery. I knew that God was there and that angels played in the rafters just out of sight. I was filled with a sense of the holy.

I also found a sense of the sacred around our family dinner table. To begin with, we never sat down to a meal without saying grace. But more than that, there was an awareness that God's grace was present in the most ordinary and everyday activities. As we passed plates of food and partook of lively conversation, both bodies and souls were fed. God's grace seeped into our daily lives. I am convinced that this is because my parents are prayerful people and ensured that we not only attended church, but also lived in faith as a family. Whether it was my mother waking each of us on Easter morning saying, "Alleluia! Christ is risen!" or my father reminding us at the dinner table to be "ever mindful of the needs and wants of others," my brothers and I were continually in the presence of prayer. Thus I believe we knew in our beings— long before we knew in our heads—that God was with us, a part of our daily lives.

I cannot say enough about the importance of family prayer and ritual in the formation and strengthening of faith. What people absorb in an hour a week at church cannot compare to what is lived and breathed in the home. Praying together and celebrating Christian rituals in the home teach faith to children, while strengthening the faith of adults.

This book of prayers is meant to be a resource to support Christian families. It is a sacred book, a recipe book, a traveler's guide, and a tool kit. Use the prayers and rituals that work for you. As you begin to pray together and to create family rituals, you will develop a style that suits your own household. Be sure that all family members can contribute in the prayers and rituals you select, even if the contribution is small.

Think of your home as a house of God, and set up your space accordingly. Just as the worshiping community of a congregation gathers in the church to pray, members of your household gather in your home to pray. Create a sacred space in your home where you gather for family prayer. For some families, this may be the dining room table or a corner of the family room. You may choose to put sacred symbols such as a cross or an icon in the space. At prayer time you might even want to light a candle or use incense to remind people that this time and space are sacred. If you're using fabric, candles, or other colorful objects in the prayer space, you can change the colors according to the liturgical season. Use purple or blue during Advent, white for Christmas and other holy days, green for the season after Epiphany, purple during Lent, white for Easter and the fifty days following, red for the Feast of Pentecost, and green for the season after Pentecost. Hanging a liturgical calendar in your home that has the seasons and holy days indicated by color is a wonderful way to help the whole family become aware of the seasons of the Church year.

While this book contains many written prayers and forms for prayer, it is important to remember that prayer does not have to be in a specific form to be pleasing to God. Prayer is about our relationship with God. Children in particular can pray in ways that are creative and profound. We use a family grace that our daughter Sophie composed when she was three: "Thanks for this food, and blessings flow. Amen." Her unique combination of phrases that she had heard in prayers delighted us with its connection of gratefulness with God's abundance. At two, our daughter Lucy often replaced a familiar bedtime prayer with a song that she made up on the spot, one that summarized her day and always included some reference to God and love. While teaching children specific prayers is easy and often helpful to them, adults can learn from the spontaneity and boldness of children's prayers. Jesus wasn't kidding when he admonished the adults to be mindful of, and to be more like, children (Matthew 18:1-7).

Enjoy prayer in your home. Celebrate holidays with Christian ritual. May your life together be a sign of the light of Christ, which others may see and perhaps even imitate.

Common
Prayer

What Is Common Prayer?

Many prayers of our faith are widely known and are called "common" for a variety of reasons. Many people from various cultures use them, so they are held in common. They are about everyday, common experiences. These prayers can be said anytime, anywhere. Chances are, when you pray one of these prayers, someone else somewhere in the world, is praying it at the same time.

AMEN

We often end our prayers with the word "Amen." Amen is a Hebrew word that means "Let it be so," or "certainly," or "truly." When we end a prayer with this affirmation, we are agreeing to the prayer, to all that has been said. Sometimes, Amen may be a prayer in and of itself. It can be our "yes" to God and God's creation.

THE LORD'S PRAYER

This is the only prayer that Jesus taught his disciples. You can find it in slightly different forms in Matthew 6:9-13 and Luke 11:2-4. The final line of the prayer is a doxology—a sentence of praise—that was added as people began to use this prayer in worship. These versions are both found in the Book of Common Prayer. The Lord's Prayer is probably the most commonly known prayer in the Christian Church.

Our Father, who art in heaven,	Our Father in heaven,
hallowed be thy Name,	hallowed be your Name,
thy kingdom come,	your kingdom come,
thy will be done,	your will be done,
on earth as it is in heaven.	on earth as in heaven.
Give us this day our daily bread.	Give us today our daily bread.
And forgive us our trespasses,	Forgive us our sins
as we forgive those	as we forgive those
who trespass against us.	who sin against us.
And lead us not into temptation,	Save us from the time of trail,
but deliver us from evil.	and deliver us from evil.
For thine is the kingdom,	For the kingdom, the power,
and the power, and the glory,	and the glory are yours,
for ever and ever. Amen.	now and for ever. Amen.

THE DOXOLOGY

A doxology is a song or sentence of praise that describes the glory of God. It frequently includes a reference to the Trinity. Here are two doxologies. The first is a traditional form that is often sung in church, and the second is a more modern version.

Praise God from whom all blessings flow,
Praise him all creatures here below
Praise him above ye heavenly hosts
Praise Father, Son and Holy Ghost

Praise God from whom all blessings flow,
Praise God all creatures here below
Praise God ye hosts in heaven above
Praise God the Trinity of Love[1]

THE SONG OF MARY

The Magnificat

Found in the Gospel of Luke (1:46-55), this is the song that Mary sang when she visited her cousin Elizabeth after Mary learned she was to be the mother of Jesus. It is traditionally called the *Magnificat*, which is Latin for the first words of the song. Traditionally, this prayer is used in the evening, on feast days that honor Mary, and as a thanksgiving for the birth or adoption of a child. It is particularly fitting to use during the fourth week of Advent.

Blessed are you among women

My soul proclaims the greatness of the Lord,
my spirit rejoices in God my Savior;
   for he has looked with favor on his lowly servant.
From this day all generations will call me blessed:
   the Almighty has done great things for me,
   and holy is his Name.
He has mercy on those who fear him
   in every generation.
He has shown the strength of his arm,
   he has scattered the proud in their conceit.
He has cast down the mighty from their thrones,
   and has lifted up the lowly.
He has filled the hungry with good things,
   and the rich he has sent away empty.
He has come to the help of his servant Israel,
   for he has remembered his promise of mercy,
The promise he made to our fathers,
   to Abraham and his children for ever.[2]

THE SONG OF ZECHARIAH

Benedictus Dominus Deus

This is the song that Zechariah sang when his son, John the Baptist, was born. It is found in Luke 1:68-79 and is often called the *Benedictus*, which is Latin for "blessed," the first word of the song. Traditionally, it is prayed during Morning Prayer, as a response to the Scripture reading of the day.

Blessed be the Lord, the God of Israel;
　　he has come to his people and set them free.
He has raised up for us a mighty savior,
　　born of the house of his servant David.
Through his holy prophets he promised of old,
　　that he would save us from our enemies,
　　from the hands of all who hate us.

He promised to show mercy to our fathers
    and to remember his holy covenant.
This was the oath he swore to our father Abraham,
    to set us free from the hands of our enemies,
Free to worship him without fear,
    holy and righteous in his sight
    all the days of our life.
You, my child, shall be called the prophet of the
    Most High,
    for you will go before the Lord to prepare his way,
To give his people knowledge of salvation
    by the forgiveness of their sins.
In the tender compassion of our God
    the dawn from on high shall break upon us,
To shine on those who dwell in darkness and the
    shadow of death,
    and to guide our feet into the way of peace.[3]

A PRAYER ATTRIBUTED TO ST. FRANCIS

While there is no evidence that St. Francis composed this prayer, it beautifully portrays the life and teachings of this well-known twelfth-century saint who gave up wealth and status to live simply.

Lord, make us instruments of your peace.
Where there is hatred, let us sow love;
where there is injury, pardon;
where there is discord, union;
where there is doubt, faith;
where there is despair, hope;
where there is darkness, light;
where there is sadness, joy.
Grant that we may not so much seek to be consoled
    as to console;
to be understood as to understand;

to be loved as to love.
For it is in giving that we receive;
it is in pardoning that we are pardoned;
and it is in dying that we are born to eternal life.
Amen.

THE JESUS PRAYER

This ancient prayer of the Eastern Christian Church
is based on the prayer of the tax collector in Luke
18:13. Its simple form allows it to be easily learned.
Some people leave out the words "a sinner." It can
be prayed at any moment during a busy day or can
be prayed repetitively as a form of meditation.

Lord Jesus Christ,
Son of God,
Have mercy on me,
a sinner.

THE BRETON FISHERMEN'S PRAYER

This traditional prayer is attributed to Breton fishermen, but for many reasons has appeal to people of all ages and occupations.

Dear God, be good to me.
The sea is so wide,
and my boat is so small.

A SARUM PRAYER

This prayer has its roots in the Middle Ages. It is a wonderful model of praying with our whole being, using our entire body prayerfully.

God be in my head.
   and in my understanding;
God be in mine eyes,
   and in my looking;
God be in my mouth,
   and in my speaking;
God be in my heart,
   and in my thinking;
God be at mine end.
   and at my departing.

PSALM 23

This is surely the best known of all the psalms, perhaps because it speaks not only of God's comforting presence but also because it acknowledges the dark times many of us face. The King James Version has familiar traditional language that many of us know, but the contemporary version that follows it, from the Book of Common Prayer, is also beautiful.

King James Version

The Lord is my shepherd;
  I shall not want.
He maketh me to lie down in green pastures:
  he leadeth me beside the still waters.
He restoreth my soul;

he leadeth me in the paths of righteousness for
his name's sake.
Yea, though I walk through the valley of the
shadow of death,
I will fear no evil:
for thou art with me;
thy rod and thy staff they comfort me.
Thou preparest a table before me in the presence of
mine enemies;
thou anointest my head with oil;
my cup runneth over.
Surely goodness and mercy shall follow me all the
days of my life:
and I will dwell in the house of the Lord
forever.

I am the good shepherd. I know my sheep and my sheep know me. As the father knows me, so I know the father, and I lay down my life for the sheep.

Book of Common Prayer Psalter

The Lord is my shepherd;
   I shall not be in want.

He makes me lie down in green pastures
  and leads me beside still waters.
He revives my soul
  and guides me along right pathways for his
  Name's sake.
Though I walk through the valley of the shadow of
  death,
I shall fear no evil;
  for you are with me;
  your rod and your staff, they comfort me.
You spread a table before me in the presence of
  those who trouble me;
  you have anointed my head with oil,
  and my cup is running over.
Surely your goodness and mercy shall follow me all
  the days of my life,
  and I will dwell in the house of the LORD
  forever.[4]

Praying
Through
the Day

Ways of Praying Daily

❧

One of the objects I treasure from my family home is a piece of needlepoint my mother made that says, "If your day is hemmed with prayer, it is less likely to unravel." This needle-work was always visible in our home during my childhood. This simple saying encapsulates for me much of what I have learned about prayer: that prayer can be a part of all aspects of our day, from work to play, to the ordinary activities that make up our lives.

There are many simple ways to add prayer to your day: offering grace at meals, blessing a child when leaving the house, remembering God while performing a daily task. Morning and evening have traditionally been times set aside for prayer. Our prayer book has formal services (or offices, as they are often called) for Morning and Evening Prayer, which are intended to be prayed by a gathered community. But prayer at the beginning and the end of the day can be offered by individuals and families as well. Morning or evening prayers can be as short as a phrase that we say when we wake up or before we fall asleep. If you find it helpful to gather as a family in the morning or evening or both, the simple prayer services found in this chapter can be useful.

⁊ Morning and Evening Prayer

These services for morning and evening are based on the Daily Office, the traditional services used for centuries by religious communities. If said as a family, you may want to gather in a special place in your home or around the breakfast or dinner table. You may wish to gather as a family in a child's bedroom to say nighttime prayers. Choose a space and a time that works for your family. Every household has its own rhythm.

Even very young children can participate in these services by learning one of the responses. In a household with small children, parents may want to introduce daily prayer with a very short version of this service, using only the opening response and a prayer. As prayer becomes a family practice, other parts of the service can be added, along with reading from Scripture.

As children get older, they can learn some of the prayers by heart. When they hear the prayers regularly, children as young as two or three can begin to recite the Lord's Prayer or a familiar collect. (A collect is a specific kind of prayer. See page 63 for more information on collects.)

Before You Begin

For prayer ritual to be effective, some preparation is helpful. First decide on a time and place to pray. Then, look through the service and decide which parts you are going to use. It is not necessary to include everything. If your family enjoys singing, include a song after the Scripture reading. A psalm or a canticle is also an appropriate hymn of praise. Some canticles include the Song of Zechariah (p. 10), traditionally used in the morning, and the Song of Mary (p. 7) and the Song of Simeon (p. 49), traditionally used in the evening.

Gather the materials you will use (such as a Bible, a song book, a candle). Choose which Scripture reading you will use, and mark it in your Bible. There are a variety of lectionaries (lists of recommended Scripture readings) available for daily use. The Book of Common Prayer (USA), the Book of Alternative Services (Canada), and Common Worship (England) each has one. You may also choose from the list below, or see the suggestions under Prayers for the Days of the Week.

Recommended Scripture Readings

In the Morning

> I Peter 1:3
> Malachi 1:11
> 2 Corinthians 5:17-18
> Romans 5:5
> Psalm 119
> Psalm 121
> Psalm 126

In the Evening

> 2 Corinthians 4:5-6
> Psalm 139:10-11
> Psalm 4
> Psalm 91
> Matthew 11:28-30
> Hebrews 13:20-21
> I Peter 5:8-9a

In the Morning

Lord, open our lips.
And our mouth shall proclaim your praise.

Glory to the Father, and to the Son, and to the Holy Spirit: as it was in the beginning, is now, and will be for ever. Amen.

Except in Lent, add Alleluia.

VENITE (PSALM 95:1-7)

Come, let us sing to the Lord;
   let us shout for joy to the Rock of our salvation.
Let us come before his presence with thanksgiving
   and raise a loud shout to him with psalms.
For the Lord is a great God;
   and a great King above all gods.
In his hand are the caverns of the earth,
   and the heights of the hills are his also.
The sea is his, for he made it,
   and his hands have molded the dry land.
Come, let us bow down and bend the knee,
   and kneel before the Lord our Maker.

For he is our God,

> and we are the people of his pasture and the
> sheep of his hand.

Oh, that today you would hearken to his voice!

A reading from Scripture.

A song may be sung.

The Apostles' Creed may be said.

THE APOSTLES' CREED

I believe in God, the Father almighty,
    creator of heaven and earth.
I believe in Jesus Christ, his only Son, our Lord.
    He was conceived by the power of the Holy
        Spirit
        and born of the Virgin Mary.
    He suffered under Pontius Pilate,
        was crucified, died, and was buried.
    He descended to the dead.
    On the third day he rose again.
    He ascended into heaven,
        and is seated at the right hand of the Father.

He will come again to judge the living and
the dead.
I believe in the Holy Spirit,
 the holy catholic Church,
 the communion of saints,
 the forgiveness of sins,
 the resurrection of the body,
 and the life everlasting. Amen.

Prayer for others and ourselves

Let us offer to God our prayers and thanksgivings
for the world and one another (name any thanksgivings, concerns for others, needs for ourselves).

THE LORD'S PRAYER

Our Father, who art in heaven,

   hallowed be thy Name,

   thy kingdom come,

   thy will be done,

   on earth as it is in heaven.

Give us this day our daily bread.

And forgive us our trespasses,

   as we forgive those

   who trespass against us.

And lead us not into

   temptation,

   but deliver us from evil.

For thine is the kingdom,

   and the power, and the glory,

   for ever and ever. Amen.

Our Father in heaven,

   hallowed be your Name,

   your kingdom come,

   your will be done,

   on earth as in heaven.

Give us today our daily bread.

Forgive us our sins

   as we forgive those

   who sin against us.

Save us from the time of trial,

   and deliver us from evil.

For the kingdom, the power,

   and the glory are yours,

   now and for ever. Amen.

THE COLLECT

O God, the King eternal, whose light divides the day from the night and turns the shadow of death into the morning: Drive far from us all wrong desires, incline our hearts to keep your law, and guide our feet into the way of peace; that, having done your will with cheerfulness during the day, we may, when night comes, rejoice to give you thanks; through Jesus Christ our Lord. Amen.

Let us bless the Lord.
Thanks be to God.

In the Evening

O God, make speed to save us.
O Lord, make haste to help us.

Glory to the Father, and to the Son, and to the Holy Spirit: as it was in the beginning, is now, and will be for ever. Amen.

Except in Lent, add Alleluia.

PHOS HILARON

O gracious Light,
pure brightness of the everliving Father in heaven,
O Jesus Christ, holy and blessed!

Now as we come to the setting of the sun,
and our eyes behold the vesper light,
we sing your praises O God: Father, Son, and Holy
    Spirit.

You are worthy at all times to be praised by happy
    voices,
O Son of God, O Giver of life,
and to be glorified through all the worlds.

A reading from Scripture
A song may be sung.
The Apostles' Creed may be said.

THE APOSTLES' CREED

I believe in God, the Father almighty,
  creator of heaven and earth.
I believe in Jesus Christ, his only Son, our Lord.
  He was conceived by the power of the Holy Spirit
  and born of the Virgin Mary.
He suffered under Pontius Pilate,
  was crucified, died, and was buried.
He descended to the dead.
On the third day he rose again.
He ascended into heaven,
  and is seated at the right hand of the Father.
He will come again to judge the living and the dead.
I believe in the Holy Spirit,
  the holy catholic Church,
  the communion of saints,
  the forgiveness of sins,
  the resurrection of the body,
  and the life everlasting. Amen.

PRAYER FOR OTHERS AND OURSELVES

Let us offer to God our prayers and thanksgivings for the world and one another (name any thanksgivings, concerns for others, needs for ourselves).

THE LORD'S PRAYER

Our Father, who art in heaven,
    hallowed be thy Name,
    thy kingdom come,
    thy will be done,
    on earth as it is in heaven.
Give us this day our daily bread.
And forgive us our trespasses,
    as we forgive those
    who trespass against us.
And lead us not into
    temptation,
    but deliver us from evil.
For thine is the kingdom,
    and the power, and the glory,
    for ever and ever. Amen.

Our Father in heaven,
    hallowed be your Name,
    your kingdom come,
    your will be done,
    on earth as in heaven.
Give us today our daily bread.
Forgive us our sins
    as we forgive those
    who sin against us.
Save us from the time of trial,
    and deliver us from evil.
For the kingdom, the power,
    and the glory are yours,
    now and for ever. Amen.

THE COLLECT

Lord Jesus, stay with us, for evening is at hand and
the day is past; be our companion in the way,
kindle our hearts, and awaken hope, that we may
know you as you are revealed in Scripture and the
breaking of bread. Grant this for the sake of your
love. Amen.

Let us bless the Lord.
Thanks be to God.

☿ Graces

A grace is a short prayer offered at the beginning of a meal. It has two purposes: to offer thanks to God for the food and to ask God to bless both the food and the fellowship. Perhaps one of the simplest ways to add prayer to your day, saying grace connects us to God. When we thank God for the food, we are mindful that all we have comes from God, that God created everything. When we ask God to bless the food and our mealtime together, we acknowledge that spiritual nourishment is as important as feeding our bodies. Saying grace also reminds us of the last supper, where Jesus prayed, blessing the bread and giving thanks for the wine (Matthew 26:26-27).

Bless, O Lord, these gifts to our use
and us to your loving and faithful service;
make us ever mindful of the needs and wants of
others, in Christ's name we pray. Amen.

The eyes of all wait upon you, O Lord
And you give them their food in due season
You open wide your hand
And satisfy the needs of every living creature
Glory to the Father and to the Son and to the Holy
   Spirit
As it was in the beginning, is now and will be forever, Amen.
                              —*from Psalm 145*

God is great, God is good,
and we thank God for our food.
By God's hands we all are fed;
Thank you God for daily bread. Amen.

Blessed are you, O Lord God, King of the Universe,
for you give us food to sustain our lives and make
our hearts glad; through Jesus Christ our Lord.
Amen.[5]

Thanks for this food and blessings flow. Amen.[6]

⁊ Blessings

When we ask God to bless someone, we seek God's
divine care for that person. In the Anglican tradition, only a priest can pronounce God's blessing on

people, but anyone can ask for God's blessing. Blessings are most appropriate for endings of prayer time or leave-taking. The following blessings may be used at the end of the day, when someone leaves the house, or when someone is about to embark on a trip.

The almighty and merciful Lord, Father, Son, and Holy Spirit, bless us and keep us. Amen.[7]

May the Lord bless you and keep you
May the Lord make his face to shine upon you and be gracious unto you.
May the Lord lift up his countenance upon you and give you peace.

—from Numbers 6:24-26

May the Lord watch over your going out and your coming in, from this time forth for evermore.

—*from Psalm 121:8*

God be with you as you go.
God be with you through this day.
God be with you as you work
and think and hear and speak and play.[8]

⨀ Bedtime Prayers

Praying at bedtime allows us to end our day reminded of God's presence. It ritualizes the end of the day. The dark and sleep hold the unknown, but bedtime prayers remind us that God is with us always. Bedtime prayers can be spontaneous or learned. Teaching children simple phrases and repeating them nightly helps to create a ritual that brings comfort and security. Some of the following prayers come from Compline, the office for the close of the day. Others are traditional nighttime prayers.

The Lord Almighty grant us a peaceful night and a perfect end. Amen.[9]

Our help is in the Name of the Lord;
The maker of heaven and earth.[10]

Guide us waking, O Lord, and guard us sleeping
That awake we may watch with Christ
and asleep we may rest in peace.[11]

Visit this place, O Lord, and drive far from it all snares of the enemy; let your holy angels dwell with us to preserve us in peace; and let your blessing be upon us always; through Jesus Christ our Lord. Amen[12]

Keep watch, dear Lord, with those who work, or watch, or weep this night, and give your angels charge over those who sleep. Tend the sick, Lord Christ; give rest to the weary, bless the dying, soothe the suffering, pity the afflicted, shield the joyous; and all for your love's sake. Amen.[13]

From goulies and ghosties and longleggitie beasties
and things that go bump in the night, Good Lord
deliver us.

—Traditional

Lord, keep us safe this night,
Secure from all our fears;
May angels guard us while we sleep,
Till morning light appears.

—John Leland (1754-1841)

THE SONG OF SIMEON
Nunc dimittis

This prayer is found in Luke 2:29-32. God
promised the prophet Simeon that he would not
die before seeing the Messiah. Later, when Simeon

met the infant Jesus at the temple in Jerusalem, he recognized God's promise and proclaimed this beautiful song of praise. It is a traditionally said at the end of the day and is called *Nunc dimittus*, Latin for "now dismiss."

Lord, you now have set your servant free
    to go in peace as you have promised;
For these eyes of mine have seen the Savior,
    whom you have prepared for all the world
        to see:

A Light to enlighten the nations,
    and the glory of your people Israel.
Glory to the Father, and to the Son, and to the Holy Spirit:
    as it was in the beginning, is now, and will be
        forever. Amen.[14]

℧ Prayers for the Days of the Week

Focusing on different aspects of faith each day of the week helps to keep our daily prayer life alive. In the Anglican tradition, certain commemorations are set aside for each day of the week. Scripture suggestions, collects and intercessory prayers (prayers for others) are included here. You may incorporate these commemorations into Morning or Evening Prayer or simply use them on their own.

Sunday: The Holy Trinity
Scripture: Matthew 28:16-20

Almighty God, you have revealed to your Church your eternal Being of glorious majesty and perfect love as one God in Trinity of Persons: Give us grace to continue steadfast in the confession of this faith,

and constant in our worship of you, Father, Son
and Holy Spirit; for you live and reign, one God,
now and forever. Amen.[15]

We pray for the Church and its peace,
for [name] our bishop and the diocese,
for [name] our parish church,
and for [names] who have died.

Monday: The Holy Spirit
Scripture: John 14:25-27

Almighty and most merciful God, grant that by the
indwelling of your Holy Spirit we may be enlight-
ened and strengthened for your service; through
Jesus Christ our Lord, who lives and reigns with
you, in the unity of the Holy Spirit, one God, now
and for ever. Amen.[16]

We pray for [name] the leader of our nation
for the peace of the world,
and for industry and commerce.

Tuesday: The Holy Angels

Scripture: Psalm 91

Everlasting God, you have ordained and constituted in a wonderful order the ministries of angels and mortals: Mercifully grant that, as your holy angels always serve and worship you in heaven, so by your appointment they may help and defend us here on earth; through Jesus Christ our Lord, who lives and reigns with you and the Holy Spirit, one God, for ever and ever. Amen.[17]

We pray for children and godchildren
[names may be listed],
for the work of education,
and for Sunday Schools.

Wednesday: The Saints

Scripture: Matthew 5:1-12

Almighty God, by your Holy Spirit you have made
us one with your saints in heaven and on earth:
Grant that in our earthly pilgrimage we may always
be supported by this fellowship of love and prayer,
and know ourselves to be surrounded by their witness to your power and mercy; through Jesus Christ
our Lord who lives and reigns with you and the
Holy Spirit, one God, now and for ever. Amen.[18]

We pray for our family and friends especially
[names],

for deacons,

for all who minister to those in need,

for all in trouble,

for the sick,

and for the dying.

Thursday: The Holy Eucharist

Scripture: 1 Corinthians 11:23-25

God our Creator, whose Son our Lord Jesus Christ
in a wonderful Sacrament has left us a memorial of
his passion: Grant us so to venerate the sacred mysteries of his Body and Blood, that we may ever perceive within ourselves the fruit of his redemption;
who lives and reigns with you and the Holy Spirit,
one God, for ever and ever. Amen.[19]

We pray for priests, especially [name],
  our parish priest,
for religious communities,
for all Christians in their vocations,
for all members of our parish,
and for the communion of saints.

Friday: The Holy Cross
Scripture: Matthew 17:24-28

Almighty God, whose beloved Son willingly endured the agony and shame of the cross for our redemption: Give us courage to take up our cross and follow him; who lives and reigns with you and the Holy Spirit, one God, now and forever. Amen.[20]

We pray for the spread of the faith,
for missionaries,
for teachers and mentors,

for godparents
and for all who witness their faith.

Saturday: Mary, the Blessed Mother
Scripture: Luke 1:39-55

O God, by your grace the virgin mother of your incarnate Son was blessed in bearing him, but still more blessed in keeping your word: Grant us who honor the exaltation of her lowliness to follow the example of her devotion to your will; through Jesus Christ our Lord, who lives and reigns with you and the Holy Spirit, one God, for ever and ever. Amen.[21]

We pray for our home,
for [names] our parents,
for orphans,
and for pilgrims and travelers.

Prayers for
People and
Occasions

Types of Prayer

When I was a child, my mother taught me about five types of prayer, one for each finger of the hand. We called it ACTIP for Adoration, Confession, Thanksgiving, Intercession, and Petition. Since then, I have come across ACTS of prayer with S signifying Supplication. Either way, the acronym reminds us that there is more than one way to talk with God.

When we pray to God, when we talk with God, we need to do more than list our wants or needs. We practice adoration by proclaiming our love for God, by noticing how wonderful, radiant, and magnificent God is. Having honored God, we then confess our sins. We tell God how sorry we are for the ways in which we have neglected or hurt God, creation, and others. Then we thank God for all we have. You'll be amazed how much you and your children have to thank God for once you get started. After we have honored God, come clean, and been grateful, then we begin to pray for others. We offer intercessions—or prayers that intercede with God on the behalf of others. We offer up our concerns. Only after we have prayed for others, do we ask God for what we need ourselves. Asking God to help us comes last.

Many prayers combine one or more of these types. A collect is a traditional Anglican prayer form. It is a short prayer that begins by calling on God, then asks God for something and ends by praising God. Collects for times of the day or the seasons of the church year are often thematic and can be thought of as prayers to "collect" our thoughts.

Throughout history, and continuing into today, Anglicans have composed collects for all sorts of daily events and special occasions. Here are some prayers you might find helpful.

For a Birthday

O God, our times are in your hand: Look with favor, we pray, on your servant N. as *he* begins another year. Grant that *he* may grow in wisdom and grace, and strengthen *his* trust in your goodness all the days of *his* life; through Jesus Christ our Lord. Amen.[22]

ON A BAPTISM ANNIVERSARY

Watch over your child N. O Lord, as *her* days increase; bless and guide *her* wherever *she* may be. Strengthen *her* when *she* stands; comfort *her* when discouraged or sorrowful; raise *her* up if *she* falls; and in *her* heart may your peace which passes all understanding abide all the days of *her* life; through Jesus Christ our Lord. Amen.[23]

FOR THE CARE OF CHILDREN

Almighty God, heavenly Father, you have blessed us with the joy and care of children: Give us calm strength and patient wisdom as we bring them up, that we may teach them to love whatever is just and true and good, following the example of our Savior Jesus Christ. Amen.[24]

FOR YOUNG PERSONS

God our Father, you see your children growing up in an unsteady and confusing world: Show them that your ways give more life than the ways of the world, and that following you is better than chasing after selfish goals. Help them to take failure, not as a measure of their worth, but as a chance for a new start. Give them strength to hold their faith in you, and to keep alive their joy in your creation; through Jesus Christ our Lord. Amen.[25]

FOR PARENTS

Almighty God, giver of life and love, bless N. and N. Grant them wisdom and devotion in the ordering of their common life, that each may be to the other a strength in need, a counselor in perplexity, a comfort in sorrow, and a companion in joy. And so knit their wills together in your will and their spirits in your Spirit, that they may live together in love and peace all the days of their life; through Jesus Christ our Lord. Amen.[26]

FOR THE ANNIVERSARY OF A MARRIAGE

Gracious God, on this our special day we remember with thanksgiving our vows and commitment to you and to each other in marriage. We pray for your continued blessing. May we learn from both our joys and sorrows, and discover new riches in our life together in you. We ask this in the name of Jesus Christ our Lord. Amen.[27]

FOR THE BLESSING OF A NEW HOME

Let us ask God to bless our home.

Jesus, King of love, you shared in the life of your earthly home at Nazareth with Mary and Joseph. Bless, we pray, our new home and our life here, that we may help each other and those who visit us to grow more and more in your love. We ask this in your name and for your sake. Amen.[28]

BEFORE AN EXAM

Almighty God, the author of all good things, who has given us the gift of minds to think and hearts to understand; be with me at this time as I prepare to demonstrate the learning I have sought. Help me to remember what I know, to trust what I have prepared, and to express what I understand. Strengthen my mind to think clearly and my heart to rest in the assurance of your favor; through Jesus Christ our Lord. Amen.[29]

FOR A GRADUATION

Gracious God, we give you thanks for all schools, colleges, and universities (especially . . .) and for those who teach and those who learn. Bless N. who has completed this current course in *her* education. Be with *her* as *she* embarks on the next stage of *her* life's journey and grant *her* many opportunities for sound learning, new discoveries, and the pursuit of wisdom. And may all *her* questioning bring *her* ever closer to you, the source of all truth; through Jesus Christ our Lord. Amen.[30]

FOR A PET

O God, Creator of all. We thank you for N., who brings faithful companionship and great joy to our lives. Bless and keep *her* in all *her* ways. And as you love all your creatures, both great and small, keep this our friend in your eternal embrace; through Jesus Christ our Lord. Amen.[31]

The litany for grief on page 80 can be used with this collect to mourn the death of a pet.

FOR A GUEST

Gracious God, we welcome N. among us.
For all that *she* brings, we give you thanks.
For all that *she* is, we offer praise.
For all that we share, we bless your name;
May we share all that we are.[32]

FOR TRAVELERS

Dear God, bless those who travel. May your word
be a lantern to their feet and a light upon their
path, that at journey's end they may safely rest in
the knowledge of your grace and protection. We
ask this in the name of Jesus. Amen.[33]

FOR THOSE ABSENT

O loving God, who has given us family and friends; be with all those whom we love who cannot be with us, guard and bless them wherever they may be, grace them with joy, protect them from all evil, and bring them safely to us once again. In the name of Jesus, we pray. Amen.[34]

FOR RECONCILIATION IN A HOME

God of peace, forgive us as we forgive each other for all the hurt we have brought into our lives. Let your healing love rest upon the wounds we have caused by our anger. Deepen our love in a new understanding for each other and for you. We ask this in the name of Jesus Christ who carried on his cross our discord and our grief. Amen.[35]

FOR SOMEONE WHO IS ILL

Most Merciful God, we beseech you to remember your child N. Send your healing Spirit into *her* body, mind, and soul. Comfort *her*, hold *her*, heal *her*. Return *her* to the fullness of life in your love, through Jesus Christ we pray. Amen.[36]

or

Lord Jesus Christ, Good Shepherd of the sheep, you gather the lambs in your arms and carry them in your bosom: We commend to your loving care this child N. Relieve *his* pain, guard *him* from all danger, restore to *him* your gifts of gladness and strength, and raise *him* up to a life of service to you. Hear us, we pray, for your dear Name's sake. Amen.[37]

FOR HEALING

May God the Father bless you, God the Son heal you, God the Holy Spirit give you strength. May God the holy and undivided Trinity guard your body, save your soul, and bring you safely to his heavenly country: where he lives and reigns for ever and ever. Amen.[38]

FOR QUIET CONFIDENCE

O God of peace, who has taught us that in returning and rest we shall be saved, in quietness and in confidence shall be our strength: By the might of your Spirit lift us, we pray, to your presence, where we may be still and know that you are God; through Jesus Christ our Lord. Amen.[39]

A Prayer of Self-Dedication

Almighty and eternal God, so draw our hearts to you, so guide our minds, so fill our imaginations, so control our wills, that we may be wholly yours, utterly dedicated to you; and then use us, we pray, as you will, and always to your glory and the welfare of your people; through our Lord and Savior Jesus Christ. Amen.[40]

For the Diversity of Races and Cultures

O God, who created all peoples in your image, we thank you for the wonderful diversity of races and cultures in this world. Enrich our lives by ever-widening circles of fellowship, and show us your presence in those who differ most from us, until our knowledge of your love is made perfect in our love for all your children; through Jesus Christ our Lord. Amen.[41]

A PRAYER OF ST. CHRYSOSTOM

Almighty God, you have given us grace at this time with one accord to make our common supplication to you; and you have promised through your well-beloved Son that when two or three are gathered together in his name you will be in the midst of them: Fulfill now, O Lord, our desires and petitions as may be best for us; granting us in this world knowledge of your truth, and in the age to come life everlasting. Amen.[42]

A Prayer before Worship

O Gracious God, whose mercies are new every morning; we thank you for the blessing of your sanctuary. Open our hands and ears and mouths that we might praise you. Open our hearts and minds and souls that we may be fed by both word and sacrament, through Christ our Lord, we pray. Amen.[43]

A Prayer before Receiving Communion

Be present, be present, O Jesus, our great High Priest, as you were present with your disciples, and be known to us in the breaking of bread; who lives and reigns with the Father and the Holy Spirit, now and for ever. Amen.[44]

℧ Litanies

A litany is a form of prayer with sentences, usually read by the worship leader, and responses, read by the congregation or the rest of the worshippers. The word "litany" comes from a Greek word that means "supplication." A litany can be used as the basis for a simple prayer service on a particular occasion. For example, the litany "For Thanksgiving" below might be accompanied by the birthday prayer in celebration of someone's birthday. When a pet dies, you could add the litany "In Grief" to the prayer "For a Pet" to honor the death of one of God's creatures. "The Cross" might be especially appropriate during Lent or on Good Friday, while "The Holy Spirit" could be used for any feast day associated with the Holy Spirit, like Pentecost, or the Baptism of Christ.

FOR THANKSGIVING

Let us give thanks to God, always and for
    everything, saying,
We thank you, God.

For the beauty and wonder of creation,
We thank you, God.

For all that is gracious in the lives of children, men,
    and women, revealing the image of Christ,
We thank you, God.

For our daily food, for our homes, and families and
    friends,
We thank you, God.

For minds to think and hearts to love,
We thank you, God.

For health, strength, and skill to work, and for
leisure to rest and play,
We thank you, God.

For those who are brave and courageous, patient in
suffering, and faithful in adversity,
We thank you, God.

For all who pursue peace, justice, and truth,
We thank you, God.

For (insert your own words here) . . .
We thank you, God.

For (. . . and) all the saints whose lives have
reflected the light of Christ,
We thank you, God.[45]

In Grief

When we are sad
Comfort us, O God.

When we are lost
Comfort us, O God.

When we are frightened
Comfort us, O God.

When we are lonely
Comfort us, O God.

When we are confused
Comfort us, O God.

When we don't know what to do or ask
Comfort us, O God.[46]

FOR FORGIVENESS

For harsh words spoken
We're sorry, God.

For silence that wounds
We're sorry, God.

For hands that hit
We're sorry, God.

For ears that close
We're sorry, God.

For gifts not shared
We're sorry, God.

For (include your own words here)
We're sorry, God.

For hearts not open
We're sorry, God.

Create in us a clean heart, O God.
And renew a right spirit within us.[47]

THE HOLY SPIRIT

Let us pray to God the Holy Spirit, saying,
Come, Holy Spirit, come.

Come, Holy Spirit, creator, and renew the face of
the earth.
Come, Holy Spirit, come.

Come, Holy Spirit, counsellor, and touch our lips that we may proclaim your word.
Come, Holy Spirit, come.

Come, Holy Spirit, power from on high: make us agents of peace and ministers of wholeness.
Come, Holy Spirit, come.

Come, Holy Spirit, breath of God, give life to the dry bones of this exiled age, and make us a living people, holy and free.
Come, Holy Spirit, come.

Come, Holy Spirit, wisdoms and truth: strengthen us in the risk of faith.
Come, Holy Spirit, come.[48]

THE CROSS

Surely he has borne our griefs;
he has carried our sorrows.
Surely he has borne our griefs;
he has carried our sorrows.

He was despised; he was rejected,
a man of sorrows and acquainted with grief.
He has carried our sorrows.

He was pierced for our sins,
bruised for no fault but ours.
He has carried our sorrows.

His punishment has won our peace,
and by his wounds we are healed.
He has carried our sorrows.

We had all strayed like sheep, but the Lord has laid on him the guilt of us all.
He has carried our sorrows.

Glory to the Father, and to the Son, and to the Holy Spirit.
Surely he has borne our griefs;
he has carried our sorrows.[49]

Prayers
for the
Eucharist

Teaching Children
to Worship

∽

When I was a child growing up in church, I thought the "Fraction Anthem" was called that because it was so short, it was only a "fraction" of an anthem. Somehow I thought part of it must have been missing. I am sure it never occurred to the adults in my life to explain to a ten-year-old that the "fraction" was the part of the service during which the bread is broken, or fractured. So the "Fraction Anthem" is what we say or sing when the bread is broken during the Eucharistic prayer.

The more we understand the liturgy, the more engaged we are in corporate worship. This is true for people of any age. The following prayers are said by all during the celebration of the Eucharist. Encouraging children to know and recite these prayers will help them to participate in the liturgy during public worship and praise God with their voices.

THE GLORIA

This is an ancient hymn, used by Christians for hundreds of years. We use it at the beginning of the service to sing praise to God.

Glory to God in the highest,
    and peace to his people on earth.
Lord God, heavenly King,
almighty God and Father,
    we worship you, we give you thanks,
    we praise you for your glory.
Lord Jesus Christ, only Son of the Father,
Lord God, Lamb of God,
you take away the sin of the world:
    have mercy on us;
you are seated at the right hand of the Father:
    receive our prayer.
For you alone are the Holy One,
you alone are the Lord,
you alone are the Most High,
    Jesus Christ,
    with the Holy Spirit,
    in the glory of God the Father. Amen.

Sometimes we use one of the following in place of the Gloria:

THE KYRIE

Kyrie is Greek for "Lord." This affirmation reminds us of God's great mercy.

Lord, have mercy.
Christ, have mercy.
Lord, have mercy.

or

Kyrie eleison.
Christe eleison.
Kyrie eleison.

THE TRISAGION

This acclamation comes from the early Eastern Orthodox tradition.

Holy God,
Holy and Mighty,
Holy Immortal One,
Have mercy upon us.

THE SALUTATION AND THE COLLECT OF THE DAY

The phrase, "The Lord be with you," is an ancient Jewish greeting. We use this greeting to call people to prayer. In worship it is used to introduce the Collect of the Day.

The Lord be with you.
And also with you.
Let us pray.

THE CREEDS

A creed is a statement of belief. The Apostles'
Creed was developed from questions that were
asked before a baptism, when candidates were asked
to confess belief in the Christian Faith. The Nicene
Creed, based on the Apostle's Creed, was formulat-
ed at a Church Council that met in the city of
Nicea in 325 C.E.

THE NICENE CREED

We believe in one God,
    the Father, the Almighty,
    maker of heaven and earth,
    of all that is, seen and unseen.
We believe in one Lord, Jesus Christ,
    the only Son of God,
    eternally begotten of the Father,
    God from God, Light from Light,
    true God from true God,
    begotten, not made,
    of one Being with the Father.
    Through him all things were made.
    For us and for our salvation
        he came down from heaven:
    by the power of the Holy Spirit
        he became incarnate from the Virgin Mary,
        and was made man.
    For our sake he was crucified under Pontius Pilate;

he suffered death and was buried.
On the third day he rose again
    in accordance with the Scriptures;
he ascended into heaven
    and is seated at the right hand of the Father.
He will come again in glory to judge the living
and the dead,
    and his kingdom will have no end.
We believe in the Holy Spirit, the Lord, the giver of
life,
    who proceeds from the Father and the Son.
With the Father and the Son he is worshiped and
    glorified.
He has spoken through the Prophets.
We believe in one holy catholic and apostolic
Church.
We acknowledge one baptism for the
    forgiveness of sins.
We look for the resurrection of the dead,
and the life of the world to come. Amen.

THE APOSTLES' CREED

This creed is usually used with Morning or Evening
Prayer rather than during the Eucharist.

I believe in God, the Father almighty,
     creator of heaven and earth.
I believe in Jesus Christ, his only Son, our Lord.
     He was conceived by the power of the Holy
        Spirit
           and born of the Virgin Mary.
     He suffered under Pontius Pilate,
        was crucified, died, and was buried.
     He descended to the dead.
     On the third day he rose again.
     He ascended into heaven,
        and is seated at the right hand of the Father.

He will come again to judge the living and the
    dead.
I believe in the Holy Spirit,
    the holy catholic Church,
    the communion of saints,
    the forgiveness of sins,
    the resurrection of the body,
    and the life everlasting. Amen.

THE CONFESSION

This general confession is a corporate prayer allowing worshippers to ask for God's forgiveness in preparation for receiving God's gift.

Most merciful God,
we confess that we have sinned against you
in thought, word, and deed,
by what we have done,
and by what we have left undone.
We have not loved you with our whole heart;
we have not loved our neighbors as ourselves.
We are truly sorry and we humbly repent.
For the sake of your Son Jesus Christ,
have mercy on us and forgive us;
that we may delight in your will,
and walk in your ways,
to the glory of your Name. Amen.

THE PEACE

Following the Confession, we greet one another with words of peace, recognizing that we have been forgiven and have forgiven others.

The Peace of the Lord be always with you.
And also with you.

THE SURSUM CORDA

Sursum corda is Latin for "our hearts." This dialogue begins the Eucharistic prayer known as The Great Thanksgiving. The word "Eucharist" means thanksgiving, and we begin this part of the liturgy ready to offer our thanks to God.

The Lord be with you.
And also with you.
Lift up your hearts.
We lift them to the Lord.
Let us give thanks to the Lord our God.
It is right to give him thanks and praise.

THE SANCTUS

Sanctus is the Latin word for Holy. This song of praise is part of The Great Thanksgiving and echoes the voices of the angels praising God in Isaiah's vision of heaven (Isaiah 6:1-3).

Holy, holy, holy Lord, God of power and might,
heaven and earth are full of your glory.
Hosanna in the highest.
Blessed is he who comes in the name of the Lord.
Hosanna in the highest.

The Fraction Anthem

The Fraction, or breaking of the bread, takes place in silence. It is often followed by a brief anthem, sung or said, that reminds us of the unity we claim in sharing Jesus' body broken and given for us.

[Alleluia.] Christ our Passover is sacrificed for us;
Therefore let us keep the feast. [*Alleluia.*]

"Alleluia" is a cry of joy. It is omitted during Lent to emphasize that Lent is a time of penitence and preparation for the great joy of Easter.

THE POSTCOMMUNION PRAYER, BLESSING, AND DISMISSAL

These forms vary from occasion to occasion. Following communion a corporate prayer of thanksgiving is said. We are reminded that we are sent out into the world to continue to spread the Gospel, the "Good News." Following are two common postcommunion prayers.

Eternal God, heavenly Father,
you have graciously accepted us as living members
of your Son our Savior Jesus Christ,
and you have fed us with spiritual food
in the Sacrament of his Body and Blood.
Send us now into the world in peace,
and grant us strength and courage
to love and serve you

with gladness and singleness of heart;
through Christ our Lord. Amen.

or

Almighty and everliving God,
we thank you for feeding us with the spiritual food
of the most precious Body and Blood
of your Son our Savior Jesus Christ;
and for assuring us in these holy mysteries
that we are living members of the Body of your
    Son,
and heirs of your eternal kingdom.
And now, Father, send us out
to do the work you have given us to do,
to love and serve you
as faithful witnesses of Christ our Lord.
To him, to you, and to the Holy Spirit,
be honor and glory, now and for ever. Amen.

Prayers for
the Church
Year

Faith Rituals
Throughout the Year

⌒

One of my richest memories from childhood is hearing my father's beautiful, resonant voice as he prayed the Advent collects at our dinner table after we had lit the candles on our Advent Wreath. These kinds of family rituals are the foundation for nurturing faith in the home. The celebrations of the church year—Advent, Christmas, and many others—provide occasions that are perfect for rituals that have been passed down for generations and for the development of new ones that your children may pass on to their own children some day.

ॐ Advent

Prayers for the Advent Wreath

Advent marks the beginning of the church year, and the use of an Advent wreath provides a wonderful opportunity for meaningful ritual in the home. Wreaths are available commercially but are easy to make as well. The wreath consists of greens encircling four candles, one for each week of Advent. The candles can be any color, but traditionally purple is used, with one rose candle for the third week in Advent. One candle is lit each day of the first week of Advent, two are lit the second week, and so on. Some people add a fifth candle in the middle, called the Christ candle, which is lit on Christmas Eve.

The Advent wreath is full of symbols. The circular shape of the wreath is meant to remind us of eternity—like eternity, a circle has no end. The candles symbolize Christ as the Light of the World, whose light combats darkness, as the winter days grow shorter and darker. The greens represent Christ bringing new life to the world. Even the colors of the Advent candles tell us something about the season: purple is the royal color of Christ our King, while the rose candle reminds us that this is a time of joyfulness.

Using the Advent wreath to mark the days of waiting until Christmas—the birth of Christ—is simple. Place your Advent wreath on the dinner table or create some special prayer place for it in your home. When the household gathers for a meal, or at some other specified time, begin by reading the Scripture selections indicated in the following pages, then light the candle or candles as appropriate, and pray the Advent Collect for that week. Be sure to include all family members in the ritual by taking turns reading and lighting the candle each night. You may wish to say the *Magnificat* (see page 7) together to remember Mary and her part in the coming of Jesus.

First Week in Advent
Scripture Reading for the Day

Sunday:	Mark 13:33-37
Monday:	Isaiah 2:1-5
Tuesday:	Luke 10:21-24
Wednesday:	Isaiah 25:6-9
Thursday:	Matthew 7:24-29
Friday:	Psalm 27:1-6
Saturday:	Psalm 147:1-12

Light one purple candle.

Collect

Leader:	Almighty God, give us grace to cast away the works of darkness
All:	And put on the armor of light,
Leader:	Now in the time of this mortal life in

which your Son Jesus Christ came to
visit us in great humility; that in the
last day, when he shall come again in
his glorious majesty to judge both the
living and the dead, we may rise to
the life immortal; through him who
lives and reigns with you and the
Holy Spirit, one God, now and for
ever. Amen.[50]

Second Week in Advent
Scripture Reading for the Day

Sunday: Isaiah 11:6-9
Monday: Isaiah 35:5-10
Tuesday: Matthew 18:12-14
Wednesday: Matthew 11:28-30
Thursday: Matthew 11:7-10

| Friday: | Psalm 1 |
| Saturday: | Psalm 80:1-3 |

Light two purple candles.

Collect

Leader: Merciful God, who sent your messengers the prophets to preach repentance,

All: And prepare the way for our salvation

Leader: Give us grace to heed their warnings and forsake our sins, that we may greet with joy the coming of Jesus Christ our Redeemer: who lives and reigns with you and the Holy Spirit, one God, now and for ever. Amen.[51]

Third Week in Advent

Scripture Reading for the Day

Sunday: Philippians 4:4-7

Monday: Psalm 25:1-8

Tuesday: Matthew 21:28-31a

Wednesday: Isaiah 45:5-8

Thursday: Psalm 30

Friday: Isaiah 56:1

Saturday: Luke 1:46-55 (the *Magnificat*)

Light two purple and one rose candle.

Collect

Leader: Stir up your power, O Lord,

All: And with great might come among us;

Leader: And, because we are sorely hindered by our sins, let your bountiful grace and mercy speedily help and deliver us; through Jesus Christ our Lord, to whom with you and the Holy Spirit, be honor and glory, now and for ever. Amen.[52]

Special Note: This Sunday is called Rose Sunday or sometimes Gaudete Sunday. *Gaudete* is a Latin word that means rejoice. Some people light a rose candle on this day. On this Sunday we remember that we are preparing for great joy.

Fourth Week in Advent
Scripture Reading for the Day

Sunday:	Matthew 1:18-21
Monday:	Jeremiah 23:5-6
Tuesday:	Psalm 71:1-8
Wednesday:	Isaiah 9:2-4
Thursday:	Psalm 24
Friday:	Luke 1:68-79
Saturday:	Isaiah 12:2-6

Light all four candles.

Collect

Leader: Purify our conscience, Almighty God,

All: by your daily visitation,

Leader: That your Son Jesus Christ, at his
                coming, may find in us a mansion
                prepared for himself; who lives and
                reigns with you, in the unity of the
                Holy Spirit, one God, now and
                forever. Amen.[53]

ℰ Christmas

BLESSING OF A CRÈCHE

Putting up the family crèche or manger scene is a delightful activity to help everyone prepare for Christmas. You may enjoy putting up your crèche piece by piece, adding a figure each day during Advent. Or you may choose to set it up all at once but only adding the baby Jesus on Christmas Eve. It is also fun to have the magi (or wise ones) travel from across the room, moving a bit closer day by day, only to reach the manger scene on January 6th, the Feast of the Epiphany. When your manger is in place, or on Christmas Eve when the Christ Child has been placed in the manger, the family can gather and say the following blessing. One person can say it, or each family member can say a verse.

SHE WRAPPED HIM
IN SWADDLING CLOTHES
AND LAID HIM
IN A MANGER
LUKE 2-7

Most Holy and Blessed One,

You sent your beloved Son into the world

as a newborn infant;

May the simple manger remind us of your arms
that hold us.

May blessed Mary remind us of your mothering
love.

May steadfast Joseph remind us of your fathering
love.

May the friendly beasts remind us of the goodness
of all creation.

May the watchful shepherds remind us of your care
for us.

May the journeying Magi remind us of the gifts we
give and receive.

May the glorious angels remind us of the
astonishing news

of the birth of our Savior.

Amen.[54]

Blessing of a Christmas Tree

The Christmas tree stems from an ancient tradition of bringing evergreens into the home during the winter months as a hopeful reminder that spring would come. It has now become a familiar symbol of the Christmas holiday. Once your family has decorated your Christmas tree, gather round to say the following blessing. One person may say it, or family members can each choose a verse. This reinforces the understanding that Christmas is a celebration of the birth of Christ.

Most Holy and Blessed One,
You sent your beloved Son into the world
    to show us the path to true life.
May the green of this tree
    remind us of the everlasting life you offer.
May the boughs of this tree
    remind us that we are the living branches of
       your love.
May the life of this tree
    remind us of the cross on which your Son gave
       his life.
May the lights of this tree
    remind us that Christ is the light of the world.
As we gather round this tree, we gather in your
    name,
    and in your light, and in your love. Amen.[55]

☗ Epiphany

The Feast of the Epiphany, the day we celebrate the visit of the Magi to the Christ Child, is January 6th. The season of Epiphany, which lasts until Lent begins, is known as the season of light. Sometime after the birth of Jesus, the magi (often known as the Three Wise Men) followed a star to find the Christ Child. According to tradition, Jesus was about two years' old at that time (Matthew 2:1-12). Because of this visit to the home of the Christ Child, Epiphany is a traditional time for the blessing of a home.

You may invite your priest to come and bless your home, or you may use the following ritual as a family.

Oh come let us adore him

A lighted candle may be carried from room to room with prayers being said for the activities that take place in that room and the people who spend time there.

This blessing may be said by the front door.

God bless this house,
From door to door,
From wall to wall,
From room to room,
From basement to roof,
From beginning to end.

God bless this house
and all who enter here,
All who eat here,
All who work here,
All who play here,
All who sleep here,
All who visit here,
All who abide here.[56]

℘ Lent

The season of Lent is comprised of the forty days before Easter. It begins with Ash Wednesday and continues through Holy Saturday, the day before Easter Sunday. Lent was traditionally a time of fasting to prepare for the feast of Easter. The forty days represent the forty days Jesus spent fasting in the wilderness at the beginning of his ministry (Matthew 4:1-11, Mark 1:12-13, Luke 4:1-13). Since Sundays are always celebration days and not days for fasting, the six Sundays in Lent are not counted as part of the forty days of Lent. During Lent it is appropriate to prepare for Easter by examining one's spiritual life and taking on spiritual disciplines such as fasting, prayer, and service to others.

BURYING THE ALLELUIAS

During the season of Lent, as a reminder that this is a season of abstinence and preparation, we do not say "Alleluia." You may wish to "bury" the Alleluias in your household. Before Ash Wednesday, make colorful Alleluia banners. Then bury or hide them somewhere in your home. On Easter day, bring them back out and display them prominently as a symbol of rejoicing.

ASH WEDNESDAY PRAYER

This first day of Lent is a solemn day. It is called Ash Wednesday, because in church we mark our foreheads with ashes. These ashes remind us of our humanity and frailness. We are called to remember that we are dust, and to dust we shall return. We are not only reminded of our eventual death but also that God created us. Ultimately, the ashes on our foreheads remind us that we belong to God and must trust in God because we are not invincible.

Remembering and confessing our sins—all that we do that draws us away from God and one another—is fitting on this day. You may chose to use the following collect in your home on this day, at Morning Prayer, or with grace, or at bedtime:

God of all mercy, you love all that you have made. You forgive the sins of all who are truly sorry. Create and make in us clean hearts, that we, humbly confessing our sins and knowing our brokenness, may receive your forgiveness and blessing; through Jesus Christ our Lord, who lives with you and the Holy Spirit, one God, for ever and ever. Amen.[57]

LENTEN LITANY

As Lent is almost seven weeks long, you may choose to mark its passing with ritual. The following litany could be used one night each week during Lent. Friday is a traditional day for fasting (which means eating less food, not necessarily no food). You might plan a very simple family meal for Fridays, and then end it with this litany.

Create in us a clean heart, O God.

    and renew a right spirit within us.

        Create in me a clean heart, O God.

        and renew a right spirit within me.

Have mercy on me, O God, according to your loving-kindness

    in your great compassion blot out my offenses.

        Renew a right spirit within me.

Wash me through and through from my wickedness

    and cleanse me from my sin.

        Renew a right spirit within me.

For I know my transgressions

    and my sin is ever before me.

        Renew a right spirit within me.

CREATE in me a clean heart O, GOD and renew a right spirit within me

Purge me from my sin, and I shall be pure;
     wash me, and I shall be clean indeed.

> *Renew a right spirit within me.*

Give me the joy of your saving help again
     and sustain me with your bountiful Spirit.

> *Renew a right spirit within me.*

Glory to the Father, and to the Son, and to the
     Holy Spirit.

> *Create in me a clean heart, O God.*
> *and renew a right spirit within me.*[58]

☞ Easter

Easter Day is the greatest day of celebration for Christians as we rejoice that Christ has risen from the dead. We understand that through his resurrection, sin and death have no final sway over us. Christ conquered them. As followers of Christ, we are promised entrance into eternal life.

After the Lenten season of fasting and abstinence, it is most appropriate to have a great feast on Easter Day. The following prayers can be used over some of the special foods we eat at Easter. Wine, bread, and lamb are traditional feast foods that date back to the time of the Exodus and the first Passover. Eggs symbolize hope and new birth, great Easter themes.

Blessing Over Foods at Easter

Over Wine

Blessed are you, O Lord our God, creator of the fruit of the vine: Grant that we who share this wine, which gladdens our hearts, may share for ever the new life of the true Vine, your Son Jesus Christ our Lord. Amen.[59]

Over Bread

Blessed are you, O Lord our God; you bring forth bread from the earth and make the risen Lord to be for us the Bread of life: Grant that we who daily seek the bread which sustains our bodies may also hunger for the food of everlasting life, Jesus Christ our Lord. Amen.[60]

OVER LAMB

Stir up our memory, O Lord, as we eat this Easter lamb that, remembering Israel of old, who in obedience to your command ate the Paschal lamb and was delivered from the bondage of slavery, we, your new Israel, may rejoice in the resurrection of Jesus Christ, the true Lamb who has delivered us from the bondage of sin and death, and who lives and reigns for ever and ever. Amen.[61]

OVER EGGS

O Lord our God, in celebration of the Paschal feast we have prepared these eggs from your creation: Grant that they may be to us a sign of the new life and immortality promised to those who follow your Son, Jesus Christ our Lord. Amen.[62]

OVER OTHER FOODS

Blessed are you, O Lord our God; you have given us the risen Savior to be the Shepherd of your people: Lead us, by him, to springs of living waters, and feed us with the food that endures to eternal life; where with you, O Father, and with the Holy Spirit, he lives and reigns, one God, for ever and ever. Amen.[63]

☾ Ascension Day

The Great Fifty Days of Easter run from Easter Day until the Day of Pentecost. However, forty days after Easter we celebrate the Feast of the Ascension. For forty days after he was raised from the dead, Jesus walked the earth, and talked and ate with his friends. But then he left them and was carried into heaven. He promised his disciples that he would be with them always, just not in bodily form. Jesus promised to send the Holy Spirit to comfort them. The ten days from Ascension to Pentecost were the true test of faith for Jesus' followers. The resurrected Christ was gone, and the gift of the Holy Spirit had not yet been received. When we honor Ascension, we honor those times in our lives when we feel lost and bereft of Jesus' presence.

Gather as a family and tell the story of the Ascension. Read Luke 24:50-53 and Matthew 28:16-20. You can hide a lighted candle somewhere in the house to symbolize that the light of Christ burns bright even when we cannot see it.

Pray one of the following Ascension Collects.

Almighty God, whose blessed Son our Savior Jesus Christ ascended far above all heavens that he might fill all things: Mercifully give us faith to perceive that, according to his promise, he abides with his Church on earth, even to the end of the ages; through Jesus Christ our Lord, who lives and reigns with you and the Holy Spirit, one God, in glory everlasting. Amen.[64]

or

Grant, we pray, Almighty God, that as we believe your only-begotten Son our Lord Jesus Christ to have ascended into heaven, so we may also in heart and mind there ascend, and with him continually dwell; who lives and reigns with you and the holy Spirit, one God, for ever and ever. Amen.[65]

☧ Pentecost

On the Feast of Pentecost, we celebrate the gift of the Holy Spirit and the beginning of the Church. The color of Pentecost is red, and the symbols of the Holy Spirit include tongues of flame, wind, water, and the dove. You can celebrate Pentecost in your home with a family dinner, using red table decorations featuring Holy Spirit symbols.

Read Acts 2:1-4.

See Litany of the Holy Spirit (see p. 82).

☞ All Hallow's Eve[66]

All Hallow's Eve, which later became known as Halloween, is celebrated on the night before All Saints' Day, November 1. Use this simple prayer service in conjunction with Halloween festivities to mark the Christian roots of this festival.

Begin in partial darkness.

Leader: Light and peace, in Jesus Christ our Lord.

All: Thanks be to God.

Reader: If I say, "Surely the darkness will cover me, and the light around me turn to night," darkness is not dark to you, O Lord; the night is as bright as the day; darkness and light to you are both alike. (Psalm 139:10-11)

Leader: Let us pray.

Lord Christ, your saints have been the lights of the world in every generation: Grant that we who follow in their footsteps may be made worthy to enter with them into that heavenly country where you live and reign for ever and ever.

Amen.

Candles are now lighted.

The Phos Hilaron is said (see p. 37).

A meal or other activity follows.

Lord's Prayer

Blessing

The Lord bless us and keep us. Amen.
The Lord make his face to shine upon us
    and be gracious to us. Amen.
The Lord lift up his countenance upon us
    and give us peace. Amen.

Leader: Let us go forth in the name of Christ
All: Thanks be to God

ॐ All Saints' Day

All Saints' Day, November 1st, is a feast that celebrates all the Christian saints, known and unknown. The Church refers to the saints as a "cloud of witnesses" (Hebrews 12:1) and teaches that all baptized Christians are "fellow citizens with the saints, and of the household of God" (Ephesians 2:19). The following song is not only fun to sing, it also teaches how each of us can be one of the saints of God. You can say or sing this hymn at the beginning of the day, or perhaps in place of grace at the dinner table. You can expand the ritual by inviting family members to dress up as one of the saints described and process while singing the hymn.

I Sing a Song of the Saints of God
Hymn by Lesbia Scott

I sing a song of the saints of God,
patient and brave and true,
who toiled and fought and lived and died
for the Lord they loved and knew.
    And one was a doctor, and one was a queen,
    and one was a shepherdess on the green
    they were all of them saints of God and I mean,
    God helping, to be one too.

They loved their Lord so dear, so dear,
and his love made them strong;
and they followed the right, for Jesus' sake,
the whole of their good lives long.

And one was a soldier, and one was a priest,
and one was slain by a fierce wild beast
and there's not any reason, no not the least,
why I shouldn't be one too.

They lived not only in ages past,
there are hundreds of thousands still,
the world is bright with the joyous saints
who love to do Jesus' will.
You can meet them in school, or in lanes, or at sea,
in Church, or in trains, or in shops, or at tea,
for the saints of God are just folk like me,
and I mean to be one too.[67]

✝ Saints' Days

Throughout the year we celebrate various Saint's Days. A list of the most well-known saints and their feast days is included at the end of this book. If family members are named after a particular saint, you may want to mark that day with prayer. The Litany of Thanksgiving (see p. 78) could be used for any saint's day.

✝ Seasonal Greetings

These acclamations may be used to greet family members in the morning, as an opening for a household gathering, or as a closing at the end of the day.

ADVENT

A voice cries in the wilderness,
Prepare the way of the Lord!

CHRISTMAS

The light shines in the darkness,
And the darkness has not overcome it.

EPIPHANY

We have seen his star in the East
and have come to worship him.

LENT

Create in us a clean heart, O God.
And renew a right spirit within us.

EASTER

Alleluia, Christ is risen!
The Lord is risen indeed, Alleluia.

PENTECOST

This is the day that the Lord has made.
We will rejoice and be glad in it.

A Calendar of Seasons
and Holy Days Observed
in the Church

✑

Advent Season

The First Sunday of Advent
The Second Sunday of Advent
The Third Sunday of Advent
The Fourth Sunday of Advent

Christmas Season

The Nativity of Our Lord Jesus Christ:
Christmas Day, December 25
The Holy Name of Our Lord Jesus Christ,
January 1

Epiphany Season

The Epiphany, or the Manifestation of
Christ to the Gentiles, January 6
The First Sunday after the Epiphany:
The Baptism of Our Lord
Jesus Christ
The Second Sunday through the Eighth
Sunday after the Epiphany

Lenten Season

The First Day of Lent, or Ash Wednesday

The First Sunday in Lent

The Second Sunday in Lent

The Third Sunday in Lent

The Fourth Sunday in Lent

The Fifth Sunday in Lent

Holy Week

The Sunday of the Passion: Palm Sunday

Monday in Holy Week

Tuesday in Holy Week

Wednesday in Holy Week

Maundy Thursday

Good Friday

Holy Saturday

Easter Season

Easter Eve

The Sunday of the Resurrection, or Easter Day

Monday through Saturday in Easter Week: the
Octave of Easter

The Second through the Sixth Sunday of
Easter

Ascension Day

The Seventh Sunday of Easter: The Sunday
after Ascension Day

The Day of Pentecost: Whitsunday

The Season After Pentecost

The First Sunday after Pentecost: Trinity Sunday

The Second Sunday through the Twenty-
Seventh Sunday after Pentecost

The Last Sunday after Pentecost: Christ the
King Sunday

Holy Days

⤶

Saint Andrew the Apostle, November 30

Saint Thomas the Apostle, December 21;
   July 3 (Canada and UK)

Christmas Day, December 25

Saint Stephen, Deacon and Martyr,
   December 26; August 3 (Canada)

Saint John, Apostle and Evangelist,
   December 27; May 6 (Canada)

The Holy Innocents, December 28;
    January 11 (Canada)

The Holy Name of Our Lord Jesus Christ,
    or the Naming and Circumcision of Jesus,
    January 1

Epiphany, January 6

The Confession of Saint Peter the Apostle,
    January 18

The Conversion of Saint Paul the Apostle,
    January 25

The Presentation of Our Lord Jesus Christ in
    the Temple, also called the Purification of
    Saint Mary the Virgin, February 2

Saint Matthias the Apostle, February 24;
    May 14 (Canada and UK)

Saint Joseph, March 19

The Annunciation of Our Lord Jesus Christ
to the Blessed Virgin Mary, March 25

Saint George, April 23 (UK)

Saint Mark the Evangelist, April 25

Saint Philip and Saint James, Apostles, May 1

The Visitation of the Blessed Virgin Mary,
May 31

Saint Barnabas the Apostle, June 11;
August 24 (UK)

The Nativity of Saint John the Baptist,
June 24

Saint Peter and Saint Paul, Apostles, June 29

Canada Day, July 1

Saint Mary Magdalene, July 22

Saint James the Apostle, July 25

The Transfiguration of Our Lord Jesus
    Christ, August 6

Saint Mary the Virgin, Mother of Our Lord
    Jesus Christ, August 15

Saint Bartholomew the Apostle, August 24

The Beheading of Saint John the Baptist,
    August 29 (Canada)

Holy Cross Day, September 14

Saint Matthew, Apostle and Evangelist,
    September 21

Saint Michael and All Angels, September 29

Saint Luke the Evangelist, October 18

Saint James of Jerusalem, Brother of Our Lord
    Jesus Christ, and Martyr, October 23

Saint Simon and Saint Jude, Apostles,
October 28

All Saints' Day, November 1

All Souls, November 2

Index of
First Lines

Notes

1   Michael Burke, from a doxology written for St. Clement's
    Church, New York City. Reprinted by permission.
2   The Book of Common Prayer, page. 119.
    Prayers from The Book of Common Prayer of the
    American Episcopal Church (1979) are in the public
    domain.
3   Ibid., page 92.
4   Ibid., page 612.
5   Ibid., page 835.
6   Written by Sophia Kitch-Peck, 2000.
7   The Book of Common Prayer, page 135.
8   Written by Anne E. Kitch, 2002.
9   The Book of Common Prayer, page 127.
10 Ibid.
11 Ibid., page 135.
12 Ibid., page 133.
13 Ibid., page 134.
14 Ibid., page 135.
15 Ibid., page 251.
16 Ibid.
17 Ibid.
18 Ibid., page 250, adapted.
19 Ibid., page 252, adapted.
20 Ibid., page 252.
21 Ibid., page 240, adapted.
22 Ibid., page 830.
23 Ibid., page 830.

24 Ibid., page 829.

25 Ibid., page 829.

26 Ibid., page 444.

27 The Book of Alternative Services, page 696.

28 Ibid.

29 Anne E. Kitch.

30 The Book of Common Prayer, page 824, adapted.

31 Anne E. Kitch.

32 Anne E. Kitch.

33 Anne E. Kitch.

34 Anne E. Kitch.

35 The Book of Alternative Services, page 697.

36 Anne E. Kitch.

37 The Book of Common Prayer, page 459.

38 Ibid., page 460.

39 Ibid., page 832.

40 Ibid.

41 Ibid., page 840.

42 Ibid., page 102.

43 Anne E. Kitch.

44 The Book of Common Prayer, page 834.

45 The Book of Alternative Services, page 128, adapted.

46 Anne E. Kitch.

47 Anne E. Kitch.

48 The Book of Alternative Services, page 123.

49 Ibid., page 107.

50 The Book of Common Prayer, page 211, adapted.

51 Ibid., page 211, adapted.

52 Ibid., page 212, adapted.

53 Ibid., page 212, adapted.

54 Anne E. Kitch.

55 Anne E. Kitch.

56 Anne E. Kitch.

57 Anne E. Kitch.

58 Adapted from Psalm 51 by Anne E. Kitch.

59 The Book of Alternative Services, pages 106–107.

60 Ibid.

61 Ibid.

62 Ibid.

63 Ibid.

64 The Book of Common Prayer, page 226.

65 Ibid.

66 The idea for this material came from The Book of
    Occasional Services and is adapted from The Book of
    Common Prayer, pages 109–114.

67 "I Sing a Song of the Saints of God." Text © 1920
    Lesbia Scott. Reproduced by permission of
    Morehouse Publishing, Harrisburg, Pennsylvania. For
    music to this hymn, see *The Hymnal 1982* (New York:
    Church Publishing, 1885).